For Katelyn Brigmon—D.D.M.

For my caring husband, Chris—J.D.

Published by Standard Publishing, Cincinnati, Ohio

www.standardpub.com

Text Copyright © 2005 by Dandi Daley Mackall

Illustrations Copyright © 2005 by Jane Dippold

Printed in China.

Project editor: Robin Stanley

Cover and interior design: Marissa Bowers

12 11 10 09 08   9 8 7 6 5 4 3 2

ISBN-13: 978-0-7847-1653-3
ISBN-10: 0-7847-1653-6

Library of Congress Cataloging-in-Publication Data on file.

MY FAVORITE VERSES

I can be happy because

GOD BLESSES ME

Written by Dandi Daley Mackall   Pictures by Jane Dippold

Standard®
PUBLISHING
Bringing The Word to Life

Cincinnati, Ohio

Even in new places,
when I'd kind of like to hide,

happiness is knowing that
my God is by my side.

Sometimes life is scary,
'cause I'm really pretty small.

But when I turn to Jesus,
then I don't feel scared at all.

God blesses those who realize their need for him, for the Kingdom of Heaven is given to them.
Matthew 5:3

Even when I'm feeling sad,
I know that I am blessed.

When the world has let me down,
I feel God's hugs the best.
If I pray and close my eyes,
I think I see God smile.
Then I let him touch my heart
and comfort me awhile.

God blesses those who mourn, for they will be comforted.

Matthew 5:4

I can help a frightened cat
who's stuck up in a tree.

I can keep from shouting back
when someone shouts at me.
I can pick up litter with a happy, joyful heart,

'cause all the earth
belongs to God,
and God gives me a part!

When someone's sitting all alone,
left out of all the fun,

It's good to say, "Come on and play!
Make way now, everyone!"

I want to do the things I should,

at morning, noon, and night.
I like the way it feels inside when I do something right.

God blesses those who are hungry and thirsty for justice, for they will receive it in full.
Matthew 5:6

At times my brother takes my stuff
or breaks my favorite toy.

I have to say that I forgive,
and then I feel the joy.
'Cause when it comes to toys and things,
I've broken my fair share.

And God forgave, so I forgive.

I guess it's only fair.

God blesses those who are merciful, for they will be shown mercy.
Matthew 5:7

Whenever bad thoughts come to me,
I try to shove them out.
I'd rather think of God and what
his kingdom's all about.

I see God in a butterfly.
I see God in a cloud.

I see God in a thunderstorm.

I hear him, too—he's loud!

God blesses those whose hearts are pure, for they will see God.

Matthew 5:8

If two good friends are arguing
and threatening to fight,
I try to help them get along;
I try to be polite.
I want to help make peace on earth
the way that Jesus did.
I'm following in Jesus' steps,

'cause I am Jesus' kid!

God blesses those who work for peace, for they will be called the children of God.
Matthew 5:9

If all my friends are heading
down a path I know is bad,
and I say no and walk away,
it just might make them mad.

It hurts when they make fun of me
for doing what I should.

But I know God is smiling down,
and that feels mighty good.

God blesses those who are persecuted because they live for God, for the Kingdom of Heaven is theirs.
Matthew 5:10

Life may sometimes seem unfair,
but God knows best,
so wait . . .

When you walk with Jesus,
your reward from him is great!

So whatever happens,
rest assured that you are blessed!

God is always with you,
and he'll see you pass the test.

God blesses you when you are...lied about because you are my followers....
a great reward awaits you in heaven

Matthew 5:11, 12

Matthew 5:3-12

³God blesses those who realize their need for him,

for the Kingdom of Heaven is given to them.

⁴God blesses those who mourn,

for they will be comforted.

⁵God blesses those who are gentle and lowly,

for the whole earth will belong to them.

⁶God blesses those who are hungry and thirsty for justice,

for they will receive it in full.

⁷God blesses those who are merciful,

for they will be shown mercy.

8God blesses those whose hearts are pure,

for they will see God.

9God blesses those who work for peace,

for they will be called the children of God.

10God blesses those who are persecuted because they live for God,

for the Kingdom of Heaven is theirs.

11God blesses you when you are

mocked and persecuted and

lied about because you are my followers.

12Be happy about it! Be very glad!

For a great reward awaits you in heaven.